Search and Find
Vehicles

Licensed exclusively to Top That Publishing Ltd
Tide Mill Way, Woodbridge, Suffolk, IP12 1AP, UK
www.topthatpublishing.com
Copyright © 2017 Tide Mill Media

1 airship

2 red diggers

3 boats

4 helicopters

5 red cars

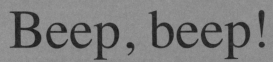

Beep, beep!

Wow, there is lots to see in this busy town!
Can you find all the things listed?

Can you find?

6 fir trees

7 cyclists

8 people walking

9 traffic cones

10 fluffy clouds

On the building site

The building site is full of vehicles digging, lifting and loading. Can you find all the things listed below?

1 yellow van

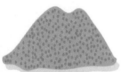

2 piles of sand

3 purple bulldozers

4 red diggers

5 cyclists

Can you find?

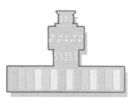

1 control tower

2 fire engines

3 blue aeroplanes

4 fuel tankers

5 yellow aeroplanes

At the airport

There is always something happening at the airport! There are aeroplanes taking off and landing and lots of other special vehicles too. Can you find all the things listed?

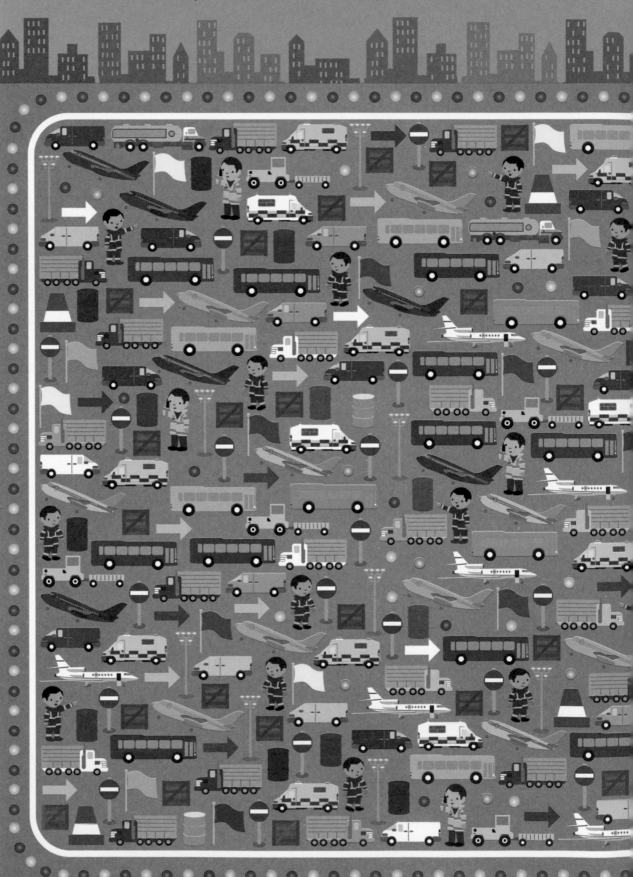

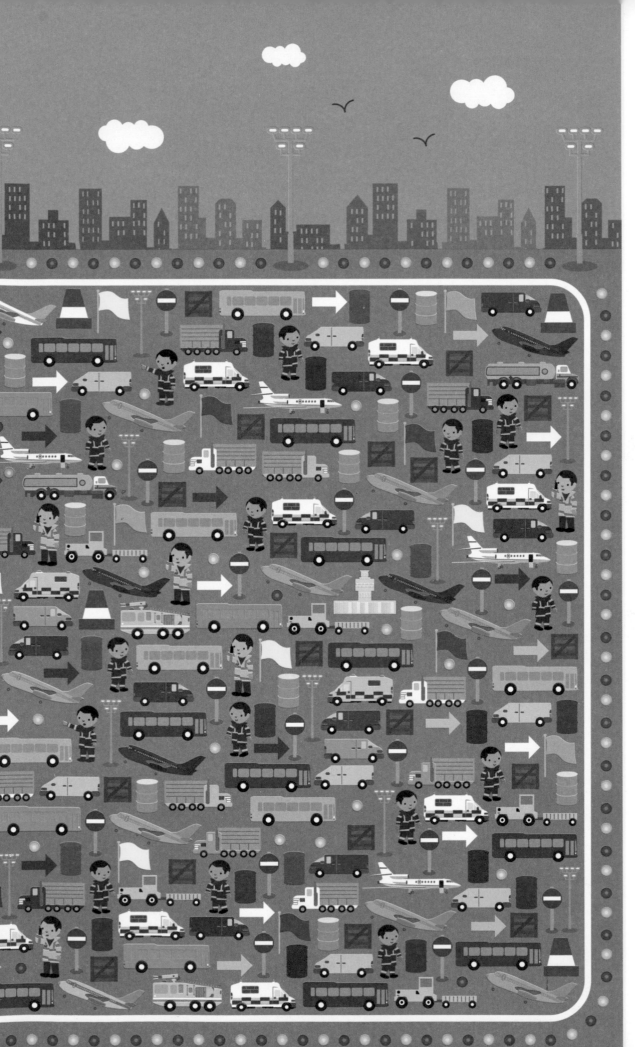

Can you find?

6 green flags

7 red aeroplanes

8 traffic cones

9 busy workers

10 baggage trailers

Can you find?

1 milk transporter

2 tractors pulling ploughs

3 horseboxes

4 combine harvesters

5 red tractors

Farm fun

Some vehicles are especially designed for work on the farm. Can you find all the things listed?

Can you find?

6 horses

7 green tractors

8 sheep

9 4x4s

10 cows

1 train engine

2 road signs

3 red buses

4 bus drivers

5 yellow arrows

Bus station search

The bus station is a busy place, full of people coming and going. Can you find all the things listed?

Can you find?

6 yellow buses

7 bus shelters

8 flower pots

9 people carrying suitcases

10 bus stop signs

Can you find?

1 lifeboat

2 hovercraft

3 ferries

4 buoys

5 dolphins

Harbour hunt

It's a lovely day to visit this pretty harbour.
Can you search and find all the things listed?

6 speedboats

7 lifebelts

8 fishing boats

9 yachts

10 flying birds

Can you find?

1 helicopter

2 tow trucks

3 piles of logs

4 fire engines

5 police motorbikes

Emergency search

Oh no! A lorry has tipped its load. The scene is full of emergency vehicles working to make sure everything is OK. Can you find all the things listed?

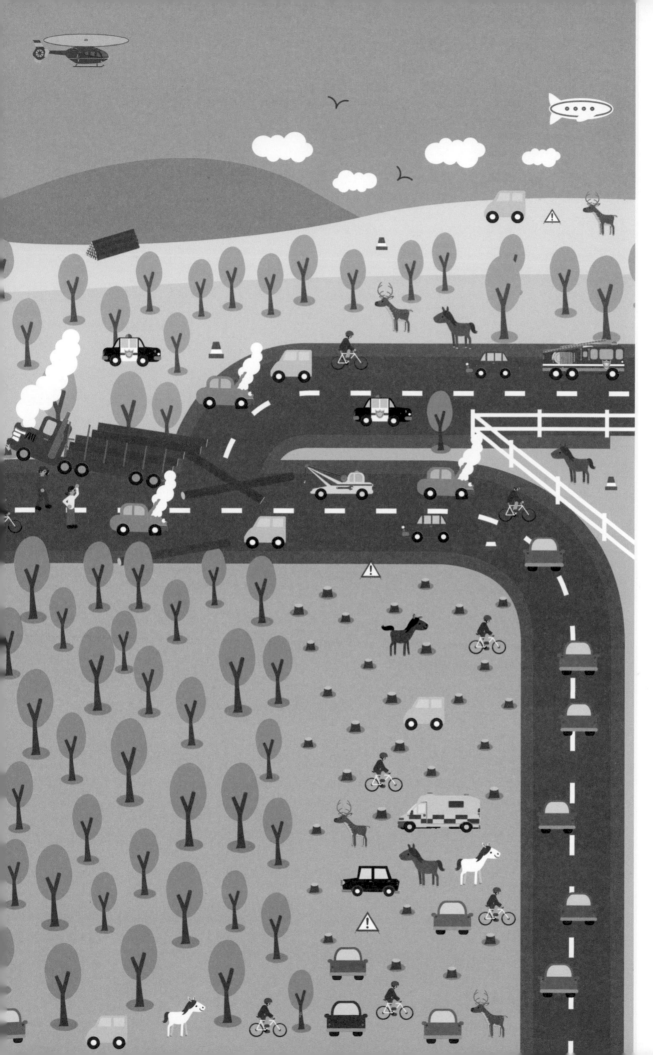

Can you find?

6 warning signs

7 police cars

8 deer

9 yellow cars

10 traffic cones

Can you find?

1 train engine

2 tugboats

3 cars

4 blue containers

5 container ships

At the docks

At the docks, enormous cargo ships are loaded and unloaded. Can you find all the things listed?

Can you find?

6 busy workmen

7 blue lorries

8 green containers

9 yellow containers

10 green and white tanks

Campsite confusion

There is nothing more fun than camping in the summer. This campsite is full of tents, caravans, mobile homes and more! Can you find all the things listed?

Can you find?

1 ice cream truck

2 sailboats

3 horses

4 blue cars

5 camper vans

Can you find?

6 cyclists

7 mobile homes

8 caravans

9 red cars

10 blue tents

Search and fly

It is the day of the airshow and there is lots for the excited visitors to see. Can you find all the things listed?

Can you find?

1 pilot

2 wing walkers

3 dogs

4 incredible flying bicycles

5 planes like this

Can you find?

6 airships

7 planes
like this

8 planes
like this

9 planes
like this

10 planes
like this

Train station

This train station is a busy, bustling place.
Can you find all the things listed?

Can you find?

1 ambulance

2 fountains

3 tables

4 information boards

5 yellow taxis

09:25

Can you find?

6 benches

7 electric carts

8 ticket machines

9 flower pots

10 black taxis

Can you find?

1 helicopter pad

2 helicopters

3 ships

4 red motorbikes

5 ice cream vans

Match day

There's a big football match, and the roads are full of all kinds of vehicles. Can you find all the things listed?

Can you find?

6 pigeons

7 palm trees

8 police cars

9 scooters

10 purple sports cars

Can you find?

**1 boat
like this**

**2 boats
like this**

**3 boats
like this**

**4 boats
like this**

**5 boats
like this**

Sailing search

The sun is out and the wind is blowing – perfect for a boat race! Can you find all the things listed?

Can you find?

6 boats like this

7 boats like this

8 boats like this

9 boats like this

10 boats like this

Can you find?

1 balloon like this

2 balloons like this

3 balloons like this

4 balloons like this

5 balloons like this

Bonkers balloons

Up, up and away! At this hot-air balloon festival the air is filled with balloons of all colours. Can you find all the things listed?

Can you find?

6 balloons
like this

7 balloons
like this

8 balloons
like this

9 balloons
like this

10 balloons
like this

Can you find?

1 orange boat

2 brown trucks

3 green tanks

4 flags

5 guards on horses

Attention!

There is a training exercise, so the soldiers at this fort are extra busy! Can you find all the things listed?

Can you find?

6 green trucks

7 helicopters

8 crates

9 wheelbarrows

10 piles of earth

Cargo chaos

At the goods yard, trains are loaded with their heavy cargo.
Can you find all the things listed?

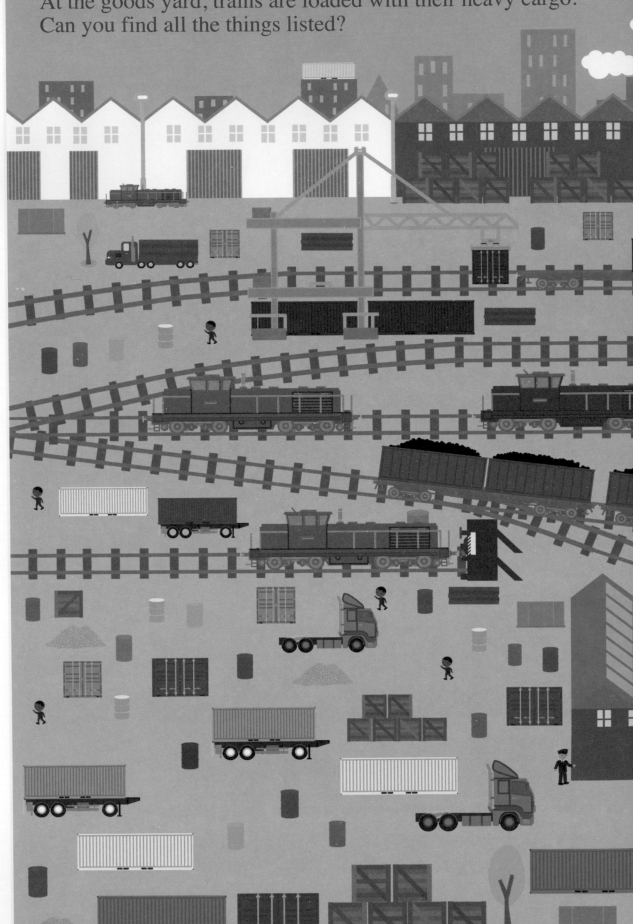

Can you find?

**1 train
driver**

**2 yellow
diggers**

**3 engines
like this**

**4 piles
of sand**

**5 piles
of bricks**

Can you find?

6 trees

7 yellow containers

8 piles of wood

9 busy workers

10 blue barrels

Can you find?

**1 ice
cream van**

**2 motorbikes
like this**

**3 scooters
like this**

**4 motorbikes
like this**

**5 motorbikes
like this**

Motorbike madness

It's the motorbike club's annual day out, and the seafront is busy with motorbikes of all kinds. Can you find all the things listed?

Can you find?

**6 scooters
like this**

**7 motorbikes
like this**

**8 motorbikes
like this**

**9 motorbikes
like this**

**10 motorbikes
like this**

Can you find?

**1 car
like this**

**2 cars
like this**

**3 cars
like this**

**4 cars
like this**

**5 cars
like this**

Classic car crazy

There are some amazing classic cars at this show. Which one is your favourite? Can you find all the things listed?

Can you find?

6 cars like this

7 cars like this

8 cars like this

9 cars like this

10 cars like this

Can you find?

**1 planet
Earth**

**2 alien
spacecraft**

**3 rockets
like this**

**4 parachuting
rockets**

5 asteroids

Space to search

Specially-designed vehicles are sent into space to perform important jobs. Can you find all the things listed?

Can you find?

6 meteors

7 re-entry capsules

8 satellites like this

9 satellites like this

10 astronauts

Muscle car madness

At the stadium, the air is filled with the noise of people cheering and the roaring of powerful engines. Can you find all the things listed?

Can you find?

1 car like this

2 photographers

3 cars like this

4 men waving flags

5 cars like this

Can you find?

6 cars like this

7 cars like this

8 cars like this

9 white tyres

10 cars like this

Can you find?

1 bear

2 caravans

3 4x4s

4 hot-air balloons

5 deer

Bonkers bikes

The steep and winding road is full of cyclists racing to get to the finish line ... but who will win? Can you find all the things listed?

Holiday horseplay

This airport is busy with people who are going on holiday! Can you find all the things listed?

Can you find?

1 pair of twins

2 electric buggies

3 red suitcases

4 electric carts

5 pilots

Can you find?

6 teddy bears

7 people wearing sunglasses

8 planes like this

9 luggage trolleys

10 hot drinks

Can you find?

1 tractor

2 picnics

3 cyclists like this

4 balls like this

5 lifebelts

Canal boat crazy

There's nothing more relaxing than a trip on a canal boat! Can you find all the things listed?

Can you find?

6 rowing boats

7 ducks

8 kites like this

9 blue canal boats

10 black horses

Search and find future

Welcome to the future! This fantasy scene is filled with cool futuristic vehicles. Can you find all the things listed?

1 cargo blimp

2 jetpacks

3 hover buses

4 hyper taxis

5 sky cars